Bring on the Funny!

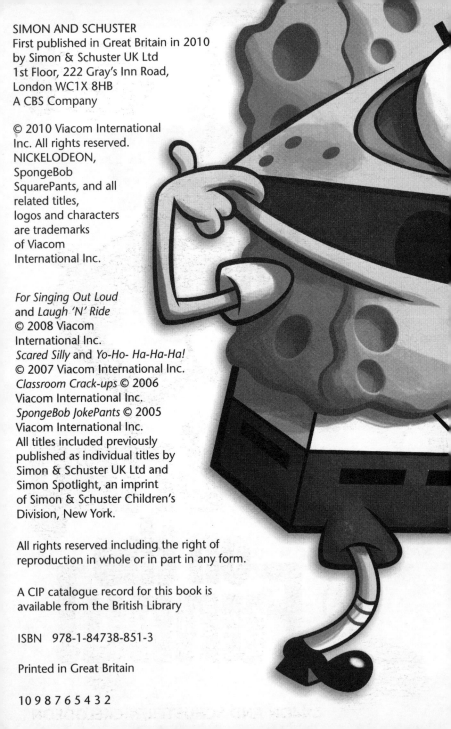

SIMON AND SCHUSTER
First published in Great Britain in 2010
by Simon & Schuster UK Ltd
1st Floor, 222 Gray's Inn Road,
London WC1X 8HB
A CBS Company

A CIP catalogue record for this book is
available from the British Library

ISBN 978-1-84738-851-3

Printed in Great Britain

10 9 8 7 6 5 4 3 2

nickelodeon

SpongeBob SquarePants

Bring on the Funny!

SIMON AND SCHUSTER/NICKELODEON

FOR SINGING OUT LOUD!

SpongeBob's
Book of
Showstopping
Jokes

by David Lewman

ROCK ON, SPONGEBOB!

- ★ **FAVORITE SONG:** "THE GARY IN THE SHELL"
- ★ **BEST MOVE:** TEARING MYSELF IN HALF
- ★ **WHAT I SHOUT AT THE END OF MY SONG:** "THANK YOU, BIKINI BOTTOM!"
- ★ **MOST EMBARRASSING TALENT SHOW MOMENT:** GOT THE MICROPHONE STUCK IN ONE OF MY HEAD HOLES

HOT TIPS

1. DO absorb a lot of water before you sing.

2. DON'T sing before you're READY!

3. DO make sure your shoes are shined and your tie is tied just right.

4. DON'T let Plankton trick you into singing the Krabby Patty recipe.

5. DO finish by floating away in a giant bubble.

Patrick: How did the traffic light do in the talent contest?

SpongeBob: He stopped the show!

Why did Mrs. Puff bake bread for the talent show?

Because there's no business like dough business.

Why did Plankton enter the talent contest?

He wanted to steal the show.

What do you call a singing contest for ghosts?

Scary-oke.

Patrick: Why did the jellyfish enter the talent show?

SpongeBob: He thought it was a stinging contest.

What's it called when SpongeBob sings at boating school?

A class act.

9

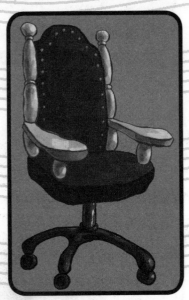

Patrick: What kind of furniture is best at talent shows?

SpongeBob: Musical chairs.

Does SpongeBob like dancing?

Yes, he gets a real kick out of it.

YOU'RE A STAR, PATRICK!

- ★ **FAVORITE SONG:** "ROCK-A-BYE, PATRICK"
- ★ **BEST MOVE:** THE BLANK STARE
- ★ **WHAT I SHOUT AT THE END OF MY SONG:**
  "UH . . . I THINK I'M DONE."
- ★ **MOST EMBARRASSING TALENT SHOW MOMENT:**
  REALIZED I WAS ONSTAGE

HOT TIPS

1. DO bring something to eat during your song.

2. DON'T mistake the microphone for a hot dog.

3. DON'T sing with your mouth full.

4. DO wear something over your underwear.

5. DO make sure your underwear is clean.

SpongeBob: Which singers are the cleanest?

Squidward: The soap-ranos.

Patrick: Who sings even higher than a tenor?

Plankton: An eleven-or.

SpongeBob: How do you make sure the audience can hear you?

Patrick: Wear a really loud outfit.

Mrs. Puff: What kind of song do electric eels sing?

Mr. Krabs: Shock 'n' roll.

SpongeBob: What kind of song do parrots sing?

Painty the Pirate: Squawk 'n' roll.

What does Plankton sing into?

A micro-microphone.

Why isn't Squidward friendly with his dance coach?

They started off on the wrong foot.

SpongeBob: Is it true that the dancers gave up?

Sandy: Yes, they threw in the twirl!

Sandy: What's the difference between a statue and an unsure singer?

SpongeBob: One's white marble and the other might warble.

Why did Plankton sweep up his footprints on the way to the talent show?

So he'd be a hard act to follow!

Why did Patrick bring a vegetable to the talent show?

He wanted to feel the beet.

Why did Patrick bring a baseball to the singing contest?

He'd heard it was important to stay on pitch.

TAKE IT AWAY, SQUIDWARD!

- ★ **FAVORITE SONG:** "I WANT TO HOLD YOUR HAND, HAND, HAND, HAND, HAND, HAND"
- ★ **BEST MOVE:** AWAY FROM SPONGEBOB
- ★ **WHAT I SHOUT AT THE END OF MY SONG:** "YOU PEOPLE WOULDN'T KNOW GOOD MUSIC IF IT STARED YOU IN THE FACE!"
- ★ **MOST EMBARRASSING TALENT SHOW MOMENT:** FOUND OUT THAT PEOPLE WOULD RATHER WATCH SPONGEBOB SWEEP THE STAGE

HOT TIPS

1. DO study classical music for years and years and years.

2. DON'T expect Bikini Bottom dwellers to appreciate it.

3. DO exactly as I do.

4. DON'T let SpongeBob talk you into practicing with him.

5. DO applaud loudly for me when I win.

Why did SpongeBob practice his arithmetic before the singing contest?

He'd heard you have to be really good at your addition.

Why did Sandy visit the Texas desert before the singing contest?

She'd heard that cactus makes perfect.

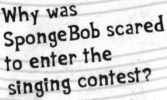

Why was SpongeBob scared to enter the singing contest?

He'd heard that first you have to make it through the dry-outs.

Why did Patrick sleep under his songs?

He'd heard they were sheet music.

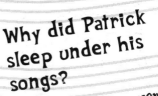

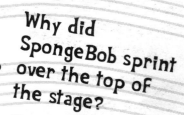

Why did SpongeBob sprint over the top of the stage?

He wanted to be the runner-up.

SpongeBob: Who's second-in-command at singing contests?

Sandy: The voice president.

What kind of tuba does Patrick practice on every night?

A tuba toothpaste.

Squidward: Why do cymbals make bad drivers?

Mrs. Puff: They're always crashing!

Barnacleboy: Why was the reporter arrested at the music contest?

Mermaidman: He kept taking notes.

SpongeBob: Why aren't stingrays good singers?

Squidward: They're always flat.

Patrick: Why aren't swordfish good singers?

Sandy: They're always sharp.

Why did Patrick bring birthday paper to the singing contest?

He wanted to be a wrapper.

HOWDY, SANDY!

- ★ **FAVORITE SONG:** "GIT ALONG, LITTLE DOGFISH"
- ★ **BEST MOVE:** EXTREME MICROPHONE-STAND TWIRLING
- ★ **WHAT I SHOUT AT THE END OF MY SONG:** "THAT ONE'S FOR TEXAS!"
- ★ **MOST EMBARRASSING TALENT SHOW MOMENT:** ACCIDENTALLY LASSOED ONE OF THE JUDGES

HOT TIPS

1. DO warm up with a cowgirl yell: "YEE-HAH!"

2. DON'T forget to wear your air helmet if you're singing underwater (and you're a land critter).

3. DO remember to smile and show your big front teeth.

4. DON'T dare to sing a song about Texas unless you're FROM the great state of Texas.

5. DO work out before, after, and during your song.

What does SpongeBob sing to his Krabby Patties at bedtime?

A lullafry.

What's the name of SpongeBob's choir?

The Porous Chorus.

SpongeBob: What's huge, stomps around, and sings beautifully?

Sandy: Tyrannochorus rex.

Patrick: The judge said I sing like a baritone!

Squidward: No, he said he can't bear your tone.

Sandy: The judge said my voice was great!

Squidward: No, he said your voice was grating.

What is Plankton calling his new store for percussion instruments?

The Drum Bucket.

Patrick: Who brings you money when you lose your horn?

SpongeBob: The toot fairy.

Did Plankton meet the dance judge's standards?

No, he fell short.

Did SpongeBob enjoy playing the trumpet?

Yes, he had a blast.

How did Patrick get caught in a drum?

It was a snare drum.

Why did Patrick build a bonfire before the singing contest?

He'd heard it was important to warm up.

Patrick: How'd the firecracker do at the singing contest?

SpongeBob: Great—he burst into a pop song.

SING IT, EUGENE!

★ **FAVORITE SONG:** "I'VE GOT YOUR MONEY IN MY HANDS"

★ **BEST MOVE:** SPOTTING STRAY COINS ON THE STAGE

★ **WHAT I SHOUT AT THE END OF MY SONG:** "EAT AT THE KRUSTY KRAB!"

★ **MOST EMBARRASSING TALENT SHOW MOMENT:** MISTOOK JUDGE'S SHINY BUTTON FOR A QUARTER AND DOVE FOR IT

HOT TIPS

1. DO eat plenty of Krabby Patties before the contest.

2. DON'T expect to get free napkins.

3. DO tell all your friends to eat at the Krusty Krab.

4. DON'T ever eat at the Chum Bucket.

5. DO celebrate winning (or losing) with a big platter of delicious Krabby Patties.

How did SpongeBob's song go over at Mussel Beach?

He got a sandy ovation.

Pearl: Why was the student disappointed with the key the judge picked for him?

Mrs. Puff: He got an F.

Squidward: What do you call a group of nervous musicians?

Mr. Krabs: A sweatband.

Why did SpongeBob's boss take up the violin?

He wanted to be a fiddler crab.

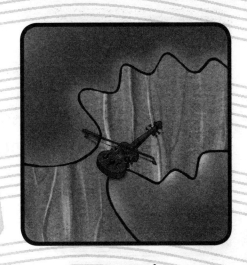

Sandy: What did the big wind tell the little wind before she sang?

SpongeBob: "Just remember to breeze."

Patrick: What kind of singing voice does corn have?

Plankton: Husky.

Why did Patrick climb up on the roof before he sang?

The judge told him to take it from the top.

Squidward: How did the mouse do in the singing contest?

Sandy: He squeaked through it.

SpongeBob: Why don't eggs sing high notes?

Mr. Krabs: They always crack.

Patrick: How did the pony do in the singing contest?

SpongeBob: He was a little hoarse.

Pearl: What musical instrument do geometry teachers like best?

Mrs. Puff: Triangles.

TELL IT LIKE IT IS, SHELDON!

* **FAVORITE SONG:** "IF YOU'RE EVIL AND YOU KNOW IT, RAISE YOUR HAND"
* **BEST MOVE:** RAISING BOTH ARMS AND LAUGHING MANIACALLY
* **WHAT I SHOUT AT THE END OF MY SONG:** "BOW DOWN AND DO MY BIDDING!"
* **MOST EMBARRASSING TALENT SHOW MOMENT:** COULDN'T REACH THE MICROPHONE

HOT TIPS

1. DO sing the Krabby Patty recipe if you know it.

2. DON'T expect to win if I'm competing.

3. DO build a remote-controlled robot to sing your song for you.

4. DON'T get in my way.

5. DO bribe the judges—but not with food from the Chum Bucket. (It doesn't work, believe me).

SpongeBob: How did the sledgehammer do in the contest?

Patrick: He was a smashing success.

Why did Patrick click his fingers through his whole song?

The judge told him to make it snappy.

Plankton: Why did the professional chef win the singing contest?

SpongeBob: He had a big range.

Pearl: Knock, knock.
Mrs. Puff: Who's there?
Pearl: Al.
Mrs. Puff: Al who?
Pearl: Altos over here, sopranos over there.

Why do chickens make good percussionists?

They're born with two drumsticks.

Patrick: Are high notes good?

Squidward: No, they're nothing but treble.

What's SpongeBob's favorite musical instrument?

The fry-olin.

Plankton: What kind of music always stinks?

SpongeBob: Reek 'n' roll.

Sandy: What kind of music is best for a ship at the bottom of the ocean?

Squidward: Wreck 'n' roll.

Mrs. Puff: What kind of music do rabbits like best?

Sandy: Hip-hop.

Squidward: What do you call a very short song sung by a cat?

Sandy: An itty-bitty kitty ditty

HELLOOOO, MRS. PUFF!

★ **FAVORITE SONG:** "MY STUDENTS DRIVE UNDER THE OCEAN"

★ **BEST MOVE:** KEEPING TIME WITH A POINTER

★ **WHAT I SHOUT AT THE END OF MY SONG:** "NOW BACK TO CLASS!"

★ **MOST EMBARRASSING TALENT SHOW MOMENT:** I WAS SO NERVOUS I INFLATED IN THE MIDDLE OF MY SONG

HOT TIPS

1. DO study your lyrics carefully.

2. DON'T let SpongeBob drive you to the show.

3. DO wear a new hat.

4. DON'T ask Patrick to accompany you.

5. DO give your music teacher lots of presents.

SpongeBob: Why are fish such good musicians?

Mrs. Puff: They're always polishing their scales.

Sandy: How did the wrecking ball do in the singing contest?

Squidward: He brought the house down.

What happened to SpongeBob and Patrick's plans for dancing on a paper stage?

They fell through.

Squidward: How is a good dancer like a stairway?

Sandy: They're both full of steps.

Mr. Krabs: Why do math teachers always enter singing contests?

Mrs. Puff: They love to do their numbers.

Why didn't Patrick take the free guitar?

He heard there were strings attached.

SpongeBob: Do guitars get teased a lot?

Sandy: Yes, they're always getting picked on.

Patrick: What has wings and plays the guitar?

Mr. Krabs: The strummingbird.

Why did Squidward play a drum for the talent show judges?

They told him to beat it.

SpongeBob: Which musical instrument is the hardest to see?

Mr. Krabs: The foghorn.

SpongeBob: Which pet is the most musical?

Sandy: The trumpet.

Mermaidman: Why do violins make good presents?

Barnacleboy: They always come with a bow.

IT'S ALL ABOUT YOU, PEARL!

★ **FAVORITE SONG:** "HOW MUCH IS THAT OUTFIT IN THE WINDOW?"

★ **BEST MOVE:** THE POUT

★ **WHAT I SHOUT AT THE END OF MY SONG:** "SIT DOWN, DADDY!"

★ **MOST EMBARRASSING TALENT SHOW MOMENT:** DADDY JUMPED ONSTAGE AND SHOUTED, "THAT'S MY BABY!"

HOT TIPS

1. DO get all your friends to cheer for you.

2. DON'T let SpongeBob come up with your dance moves.

3. DO wear your hair in a ponytail.

4. DO throw an after-party.

5. DON'T throw it at the Krusty Krab.

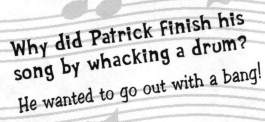

Why did Patrick finish his song by whacking a drum?

He wanted to go out with a bang!

nickelodeon

SpongeBob SQUAREPANTS

Scared Silly!

SpongeBob's Book of
Spooky Jokes

by David Lewman

Who's yellow, porous, and spooky?

SpongeBob ScarePants!

Boo!

Boo!

What happened to SpongeBob after Sandy told him a spooky story about cows?

He kept having night*moo*-ers.

Boo!

Boo! *Boo!*

What's the difference between SpongeBob's pet and a ghostly claw?

One's a snail named Gary, and the other's a nail that's scary.

Boo!

Boo!

What does Sandy call a scary dream about acorns?

A *nut*mare.

Boo!

Boo!

Boo!

What's the difference between a ghost's handshake and Mr. Krabs?

One's a creepy grab, and the other's a greedy crab.

What do monsters shout out at midnight on December 31?

"Happy New Fear!"

SpongeBob: Are sea fossils ever scared?

Squidward: They're more than scared—they're petrified!

Sandy: Did the ghosts like each other?

Pearl: Oh, yes, it was love at first fright.

SpongeBob: Where do you go to mail a letter to a ghoul?

Mrs. Puff: The ghost office.

Patrick: Which plant do ghosts like best?

Plankton: Bam*boo*!

Sandy: What do ghosts use to wash their hair?

SpongeBob: Sham*boo*!

Why is Mr. Krabs afraid of ghosts?

He's afraid they'll go through his wallet.

Why did Plankton hire a ghost chef?

It could always scare up something to eat.

Patrick: What do ghosts love to play at parties?

Pearl: Musical scares!

SpongeBob: Why did the fish act brave around the fisherman?

Plankton: He didn't want to look like a scaredy-catch.

Does the Flying Dutchman ever leave Bikini Bottom without scaring anyone?

No, he won't give up without a fright.

What did SpongeBob say when the ghoul wanted to haunt his house?

"Be my ghost!"

SpongeBob: When's the best time to look through a phantom?

Mermaid Man: When the ghost is clear.

Patrick: Why did the spirit haunt the TV station?

Sandy: He wanted to be a talk-show ghost.

Mr. Krabs: What colors are on the ghost flag?

Squidward: Red, white, and *boo!*

63

Patrick: What do you get when you cross a fish and a giant dinosaur?

Plankton: *Codzilla.*

Patrick: What do ghosts sing to their babies?

SpongeBob: Lulla*boo*s.

Squidward: What did the ghost say to the wall?

Sandy: "Just passing through."

What's the difference between a ghost and Plankton?

One's a floating ghoul, and the other's a gloating fool.

Mermaid Man: What do spiders eat at picnics?

Sandy: Corn on the cobweb.

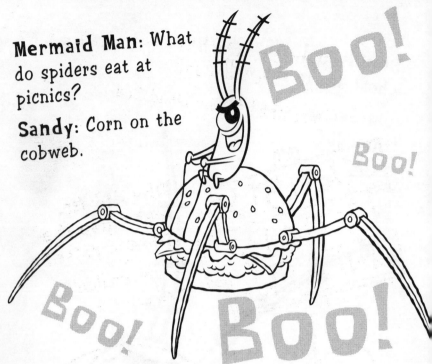

SpongeBob: Which snake gives the prettiest presents?

Sandy: The bow constrictor.

Patrick: Which sea is the most haunted?

Mr. Krabs: The Dead Sea.

Why did Mr. Krabs give the snake a raise?

So he wouldn't strike.

Boo!

Boo!

Boo!

Boo!

KRUSTY KRAB UNFAIR

Patrick: Did SpongeBob do a good job entertaining the ghosts?

Sandy: Yes, sirree, he knocked 'em dead.

Sandy: What do you call two ghosts who just got married?

Squidward: Newlydeads.

Squidward: What do ghosts say to each other at breakfast?

Mr. Krabs: "Good moaning!"

Why did Patrick aim a big fan at the ghosts?

He wanted to keep his spirits up.

69

Pearl: What do you get when you cross a ghost with a girl's shirt?

Sandy: A haunted blouse.

Sandy: What do hairdressers get when they're scared?

Pearl: Moussebumps.

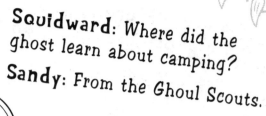

Squidward: Where did the ghost learn about camping?

Sandy: From the Ghoul Scouts.

Patrick: What kind of TVs do ghosts have?

Squidward: Wide scream.

What's the difference between a ghost and Plankton?

One loves to make you scream, and the other loves to make new schemes.

SpongeBob: Why did the spider put her web on the road?

Patrick: She wanted to go for a spin.

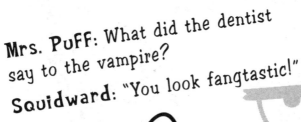

Mr. Krabs: What do monsters eat for breakfast?

SpongeBob: Peaches and scream.

Mrs. Puff: What did the dentist say to the vampire?

Squidward: "You look fangtastic!"

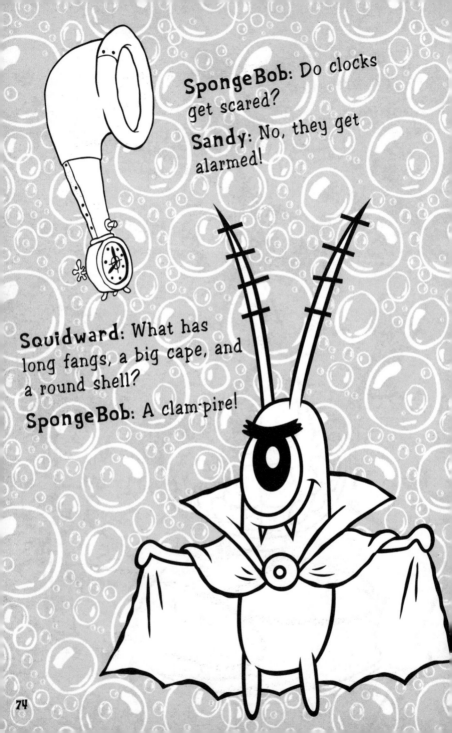

SpongeBob: Do clocks get scared?

Sandy: No, they get alarmed!

Squidward: What has long fangs, a big cape, and a round shell?

SpongeBob: A clam-pire!

Why did SpongeBob think Mrs. Puff was going to catch a chief vampire?

She said she was going to take a head count.

Sandy: When's the best time to catch vampire fish?

SpongeBob: When they're not biting.

Mr. Krabs: How did Dracula do in the vampire race?

Squidward: He won by a neck.

Boo!

Boo!

Boo!

When is Squidward like a vampire?

When he's a pain in the neck.

Boo! Boo! Boo!

Patrick: What did the vampire say as he fell in the ocean?

Sandy: "I want to suck your . . . blub . . . blub . . . blub . . ."

What does SpongeBob turn into whenever the moon is full?

A squarewolf.

Plankton: What's white and tight and turns hairy when the moon is full?

Patrick: An underwearwolf.

Patrick: When do sheep turn into were-sheep?

Squidward: Whenever there's a wool moon.

SpongeBob: Why was the werewolf thrown out of the basketball game?

Pearl: For a technical howl.

Who haunts the Seven Seas and is great at jumping rope?

The Flying Double-Dutchman.

Mr. Krabs: Which monster is big and green and complains a lot?

Squidward: Frankenwhine.

SpongeBob: What's the difference between a fisherman and a witch?

Mrs. Puff: One casts hooks, and the other casts a hex.

Mr. Krabs: What do you get when you cross a witch and a dinosaur?

Squidward: Tyrannosaurus Hex.

Sandy: What's the difference between a purse and a witch who plays an instrument?

Mrs. Puff: One's a handbag, and the other's a band hag.

SpongeBob: Who always comes right after the aliens?

Patrick: The *b*-liens.

SpongeBob: Why are aliens so weird?

Patrick: Uh, maybe because they come from odder space.

82

Patrick: How do alien potatoes travel?

SpongeBob: In a space chip.

Sandy: Where do alien fish come from?

Mr. Krabs: Chowder space.

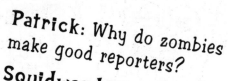

Sandy: Did the zombie enjoy the graveyard party?

SpongeBob: Yes, he had the tomb of his life.

Patrick: Why do zombies make good reporters?

Squidward: They always meet their deadlines.

SpongeBob: What's the difference between a funeral director and a pirate?

Mr. Krabs: One's an undertaker, and the other's a plunder taker.

Patrick: Why did the vampire fly into the bell?

Squidward: He wanted to be a dingbat.

SpongeBob: Are vampires loyal?

Mr. Krabs: Yes, they'll always go to bat for you.

Boo!

Boo!

Boo!

SpongeBob: Why did the vampire fly to the baseball field?

Sandy: It was his turn at bat.

Boo!

Boo!

Why did Patrick try to rescue the Egyptian queen from her tomb?

He'd heard Mr. Krabs say you should always save your mummy.

Patrick: Why are mummies wrapped in bandages?

Squidward: Oh, just be gauze, Patrick.

Boo! Boo! Boo! Boo! Boo!

Pearl: What happened to the young mummy who misbehaved?

Mrs. Puff: He got sent to his tomb.

SpongeBob: What kind of music do mummies like?

Squidward: Wrap.

Which spooky story is about a mad scientist who turns himself into a Krabby Patty?

"Dr. Jekyll and Mr. Fried."

Why did Patrick bring a mechanical man along in his boat?

He thought it was a row-bot.

Boo! Boo!

Mrs. Puff: Why was the skeleton late to school?

Sandy: Her dog kept burying her!

Boo! Boo!

What does Squidward have under his skin?

A scowl-eton.

Boo!

Boo!

SpongeBob: What's a skeleton's favorite dessert?

Patrick: Chocolate bone-bones.

Boo!

Boo!

Sandy: Why couldn't the skeleton fall in love?

Mrs. Puff: He had a heart of bone.

Boo!

SpongeBob: How do you know if you're a skeleton?

Squidward: You feel it in your bones.

Why did the skeleton take so many towels to Goo Lagoon?

He wanted to stay bone-dry.

SpongeBob: What's covered in wool and full of aliens?

Sandy: A Ewe-F-O.

Patrick: Who wears a black robe and smells terrible?

Squidward: The Grim Reeker.

SpongeBob: Who wears a black robe and makes up great rhymes?

Sandy: The Grim Rapper.

Squidward: Why was the skeleton constantly arguing?

Mr. Krabs: He always had a bone to pick with someone.

Pearl: Which vampire feels at home in the water?

Plankton: Count Quackula.

What scary creature lives under Patrick's bed?

The Loch Mess Monster.

How did SpongeBob feel when a face appeared in his bowl of Kelpo?

A chill ran up his spoon.

Why does Patrick think darkness is heavy?

Because it isn't light.

Why did Patrick think Squidward's nose was scared?

It was running.

Mr. Krabs: When is a fisherman spooky?

SpongeBob: When he casts a shadow.

SpongeBob
JokePants

by David Lewman

What would you call Gary if he lived on a farm?

"The Farmer in the Shell."

What's SpongeBob's favorite kind of knot?

The square knot.

What kind of shoes does SpongeBob wear?

Penny loofahs.

103

Was Squidward mad when
SpongeBob jumped on his mop?

Yes, he flew off the handle.

Why couldn't Plankton pay
for his Krabby Patty?

He was a little short.

What side order does Sandy always get with her Krabby Patty?

Squirrelly fries.

What does SpongeBob do when Squidward drops food?

He goes on a mopping spree!

What does Mr. Krabs like best about SpongeBob?

His buck teeth.

How does Mr. Krabs start every bedtime story?

"Once upon a dime . . ."

What's Mr. Krabs's favorite kind of bread?

Pumper-nickel.

What kind of nuts does Mr. Krabs like the best?

Cash-ews.

What do you see when Mr. Krabs's daughter smiles?

Her Pearly whites.

Why did SpongeBob fail his boating test?

He forgot to fasten his sea belt.

Mrs. Puff: Knock-knock.
SpongeBob: Who's there?
Mrs. Puff: Teach.
SpongeBob: Teach who?
Mrs. Puff: Teach yourself
       to drive—I give up!

RULES of the ROAD

What does every restaurant get when SpongeBob's behind the wheel?

A drive-through.

109

Patrick: What do sponges
play at their
birthday parties?
SpongeBob: Musical squares.

What game does SpongeBob
play with his shoes?
Hide-and-squeak.

Why did SpongeBob tear himself in half at the end of the party?

Because Sandy said it was time to split.

Why did SpongeBob wash the reef?

He was practicing good coral hygiene.

Is Plankton nice to the reefs around Bikini Bottom?

No, he's rotten to the coral.

How do angelfish greet each other?

"Halo!"

Why does Sandy's fur stand up on end whenever Plankton's around?

He rubs her the wrong way.

Where do Sandy and SpongeBob
practice their karate?

In choppy water.

Sandy: What kind of pizza do
they serve at the
bottom of the ocean?
SpongeBob: Deep dish.

What kind of earrings does
Sandy's mom wear?

Mother-of-squirrel.

What do you get when you cross a squid and a dog?

An octo-pooch.

What do you get when
you cross a hunting dog,
a seagull, and a bumblebee?

A *bee-gull.*

Why can't Sandy play on Patrick's basketball team?

Because he's on an all-star team.

Why did Patrick stare at a mirror with his mouth open?

Squidward told him to watch his tongue.

What's salty and feels good on a sunburn?

The Pacific Lotion.

Is Patrick happy with the way he looks?

Yes, he's tickled pink!

What makes Patrick grouchy?

Waking up on the wrong side of the rock.

Why did SpongeBob chop the joke book in half?

Squidward told him to cut the comedy.

What's the most popular hobby in Bikini Bottom?

Damp collecting!

How did Squidward do in the hundred-yard dash?

He won by a nose.

118

What kind of ocean bird can't fly, can't swim, and can't catch fish?

A peli-can't.

What did SpongeBob yell when he dressed up as a bear?

"I'm Teddy!"

Squidward: Why does Gary meow?
SpongeBob: Because he doesn't know how to bark!

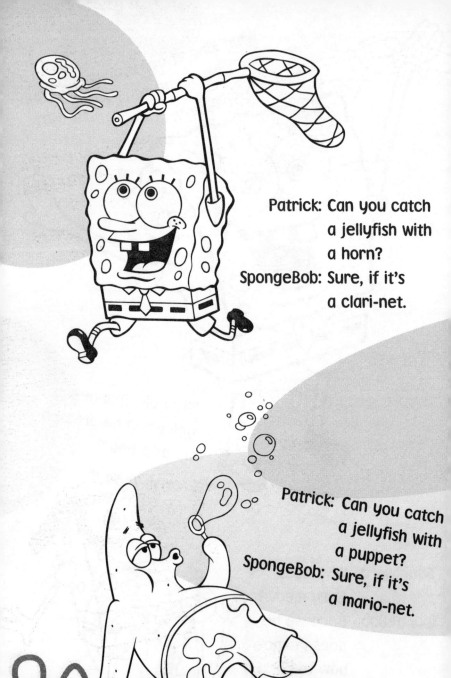

Patrick: Can you catch a jellyfish with a horn?

SpongeBob: Sure, if it's a clari-net.

Patrick: Can you catch a jellyfish with a puppet?

SpongeBob: Sure, if it's a mario-net.

Why can't seahorses agree
on new rules?

*They always vote
neigh.*

What's the difference between
SpongeBob and a gold chain?

*One's a yellow necklace, and the
other's yellow and neck-less.*

If Sandy were a tree, what kind would she be?

A fur tree.

SpongeBob: Why can't an eel ever win an argument?

Sandy: It doesn't have a leg to stand on.

123

Why did SpongeBob practice his karate at the Krusty Krab?

He thought he was supposed to punch in and punch out.

Where do crabs take classes?

Claw school.

What's Mr. Krabs's favorite chore?

Taking out the cash.

Does SpongeBob have a good time at work?

Yes, he's the life of the patty.

What do Krabby Patties and long hair have in common?

They both fit in a bun.

Patrick: What do jellyfish
eat for breakfast?
SpongeBob: Floatmeal!

SpongeBob: What has two big
claws and is very
messy?
Patrick: A slobster!

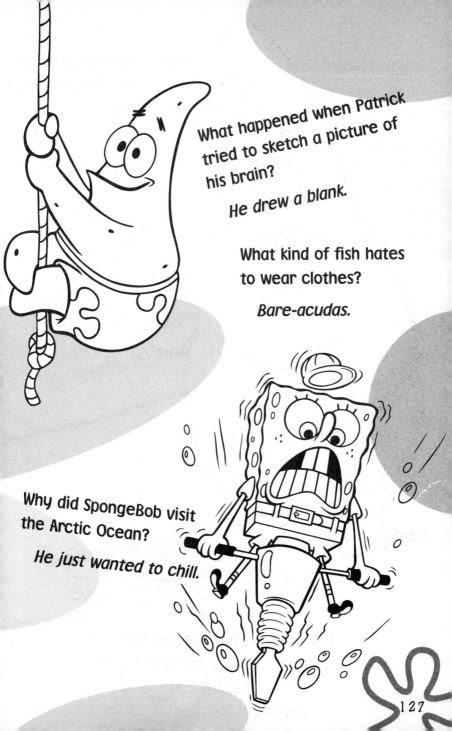

What happened when Patrick tried to sketch a picture of his brain?

He drew a blank.

What kind of fish hates to wear clothes?

Bare-acudas.

Why did SpongeBob visit the Arctic Ocean?

He just wanted to chill.

127

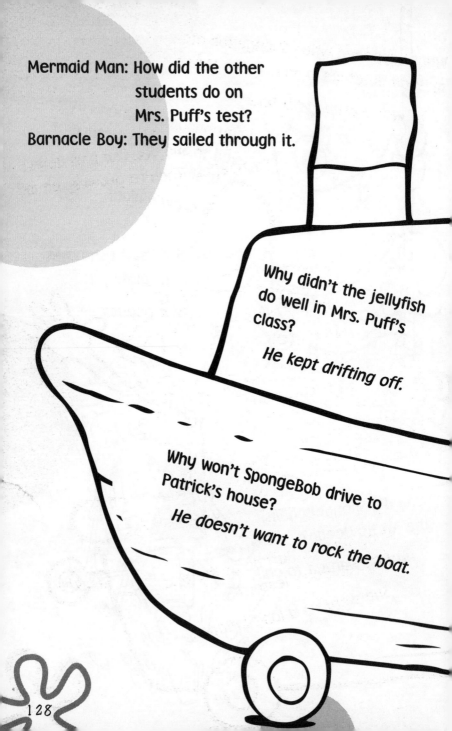

Mermaid Man: How did the other
students do on
Mrs. Puff's test?
Barnacle Boy: They sailed through it.

Why didn't the jellyfish
do well in Mrs. Puff's
class?

He kept drifting off.

Why won't SpongeBob drive to
Patrick's house?

He doesn't want to rock the boat.

What happened when SpongeBob ate
mashed potatoes in Mrs. Puff's class?

He got a lump in his boat.

Patrick: Do you like barnacles?
SpongeBob: They're growing on me.

What did Mrs. Puff do at the end
of SpongeBob's lesson?

She went on a long inflation.

Patrick: What's Plankton's favorite dessert?
SpongeBob: Shortcake.

If Patrick's best friend were a dessert, what kind would he be?

Sponge cake.

Why would Mr. Krabs like to be a bowl of chocolate ice cream?

Because it's very rich.

Patrick: Who haunts the seven seas but never vacuums?

SpongeBob: The Flying Dustman!

Mermaid Man: What does it take to get into a fish choir?

Barnacle Boy: You have to be able to carry a tuna.

Why did Patrick pull the ship with a rope?

He'd heard it was a tugboat.

Where would SpongeBob live
after an earthquake?

In a pineapple upside-down
house.

What do you call someone who
just sits around blowing into a
shell?

A conch potato!

Why didn't SpongeBob's pants
fall down during the hurricane?

He was saved by the belt.

Sandy: Why didn't the boy penguin ask the girl penguin out on a date?

SpongeBob: He got cold feet.

How is Sandy able to get around Bikini Bottom without getting wet?

She has her dry-fur's license.

Why did the police arrest Gary?

He was found at the scene of the slime.

Knock-knock.
Who's there?
Hatch.
Hatch who?
Gesundheit!

Squidward: Knock-knock.
SpongeBob: Who's there?
Squidward: Claire.
SpongeBob: Claire who?
Squidward: Clarinets sound
            beautiful,
            don't they?

Why does Mr. Krabs have so many clocks in his house?

Because time is money.

Why does Mr. Krabs like to mop up?

Because inside every bucket, there's a buck.

Why did SpongeBob put his ear to the cash register?

Because Mr. Krabs told him, "Money talks."

Was Mr. Krabs mad when SpongeBob dropped the butter?

No, he let it slide.

What do you call Mr. Krabs when he's holding a coin?

A penny-pincher.

How does SpongeBob get exercise?

He does deep-sea bends.

Why did the quilt refuse to go to Bikini Bottom?

She didn't want to be a wet blanket.

What does SpongeBob
sleep in?

His under-square.

Where do sea cows
sleep at night?

In the barn-acle.

Squidward: Why do starfish get up
in the middle of the night?

SpongeBob: They have to twinkle.

How do you save jellyfish from drowning?

Throw them some life preserves.

Why couldn't Patrick understand what the jellyfish was saying?

It was way over his head.

Why did SpongeBob toss the sandwich at Patrick?

He wanted to throw him a surprise patty.

SpongeBob: What has horns, four legs,
and is made out of soap?
Sandy: A bubbalo!

When is SpongeBob like a battery?

When *he gets all charged up!*

Why doesn't SpongeBob
go to the barber?

He doesn't like to cut
corners.

Why do SpongeBob and Sandy
surf so well together?

They're on the same
wavelength.

What did Sandy say when she finished gathering acorns?

"That's all, oaks!"

How does Sandy feel about SpongeBob?

She's nuts about him!

What's SpongeBob's favorite last-minute Halloween costume?

Swiss cheese.

The End.

Laugh 'n' Ride

A SpongeBob Joke Book

by David Lewman

SpongeBob ran up to Patrick's rock. "Patrick!" he called. "It's time for the Annual Jellyfishing Convention! We're going on a trip!"

"Oh, boy! A trip!" cried Patrick. "Let's go RIGHT NOW!"

SpongeBob smiled. "Hold on, Patrick. First we have to pack."

"Uh . . . what do we have to pack?" asked Patrick.

"Well, let's see . . . underwear, toothbrush, pajamas . . . ," SpongeBob started to say.

"That doesn't sound like fun, SpongeBob," Patrick said.

"Yeah, but we can tell each other jokes while we pack!" SpongeBob said. "Like this one: What did the little sponge keep asking his parents on their trip?"

"I dunno . . . ," said Patrick.

"Are we square yet?" answered SpongeBob, and the two friends cracked up. "Now it's your turn."

"Uh . . . what kind of pants can you make out of a suitcase?" asked Patrick. Before SpongeBob could answer, Patrick excitedly shouted out, "Baggy pants! Get it?"

So SpongeBob and Patrick packed their backpacks and told jokes.

Why did the duck miss his bus?

He was up all night quacking.

QUACK!
QUACK!
QUACK!

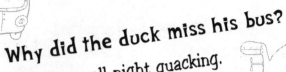

What does Gary pack before a trip?

His sluggage.

Where does Mr. Krabs keep his bags?

Under his eyes.

Why was the clown up late the night before his trip?

He was packing his gags.

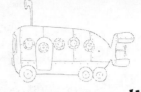

What do traveling dogs carry their clothes in?

Barkpacks.

What do you say when you can't decide whether to travel or pig out?

"Trip or treat!"

Why didn't Mrs. Puff visit the puzzle museum?

She didn't want to go to pieces.

What do cows like to visit on their vacations?

The *mooseums*.

Which part of a trip do combs like best?

Departing.

Why did the ice cream keep diving into the root beer?

He loved to fizz it!

Why did the tourist visit haunted houses?

He loved frightseeing.

THREE HOURS LATER

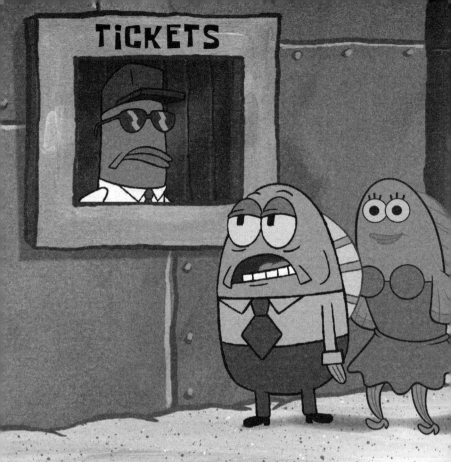

Once they had packed their backpacks, SpongeBob and Patrick went to the Bikini Bottom bus station to buy tickets. But when they got to the station, there was a long line of fish waiting at the ticket window.

"Oh no, SpongeBob, we're going to have to wait in line forever!" Patrick whined.

"Don't worry, Patrick," SpongeBob asked. "We could do something fun."

Patrick grinned. "Like build a house of cards?"

"Or tell each other more jokes!" SpongeBob said.
"Knock, knock."

"Who's there?" answered Patrick.

"Sleeve."

"Sleeve who?"

"Let's leave and go on a trip!" SpongeBob shouted, and the pair laughed and laughed till they both teared up. Even some of the folks in line giggled.

SpongeBob and Patrick started to trade more jokes.

Why did the traveler wad his boarding pass up into a ball?

He wanted a round-trip ticket.

Why don't bowlers mind flat tires?

They can always get a spare.

What do ghosts buy when they travel?
Boo-venirs.

What do mosquitoes write when they go on vacation?

Pestcards.

Why did the tourist punch the street?

He wanted to hit the road.

What do you call a pig running down a highway?

A road hog.

Why did Mrs. Puff's class keep letting all the other classes go first?

They were on a yield trip.

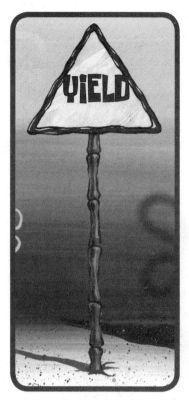

How did the road feel when a potato snack landed on it?

Like it had a chip on its shoulder.

What's the difference between a concrete path and a big stocking?

One's a sidewalk and the other's a wide sock.

What's the difference between a tour book and a wave full of pebbles?

One's a travel guide and the other's a gravel tide.

TEN
HOURS
LATER

SpongeBob even had the guy at the ticket window laughing when he told this joke. "Why did the traveler wear his swimsuit for the road trip?" asked SpongeBob.

The ticket-window guy shrugged.

"He'd heard they were going in a carpool!" SpongeBob said, and everyone clapped.

"That was funny," the ticket-window guy said. "And just for making me laugh, you get two tickets for the price of one."

Patrick and SpongeBob couldn't believe it. "Thanks!" they said.

They climbed up the steps of the bus that would take them to the convention, and found seats in the back. After about two minutes Patrick asked, "Are we square yet? I mean, are we there yet? Ha-ha-ha-ha!"

"Nope," said SpongeBob. "It's going to be a while before we get to the convention."

"Auggghhh!" Patrick groaned. "Long drives are BORING!"

"Not if we tell each other certain somethings," SpongeBob said, giggling.

"Like what?" Patrick asked.

"Jokes!" answered SpongeBob.

How did the pair of penguins travel?

On an icicle built for two.

Why did Sandy slide down the mountain on her vacation?

She wanted to go sight-skiing.

When is a wave like a car coming to a stop?

When it breaks.

Why did the actor refuse to slow down until the end of her trip?

She was waiting for her big brake.

Why did Mr. Krabs cover his lawn with a white canvas?

He wanted to have a yard sail.

Which oar is no good For rowing a boat?

A dinosaur.

What do you call it when two oars fall in love?

True row-mance.

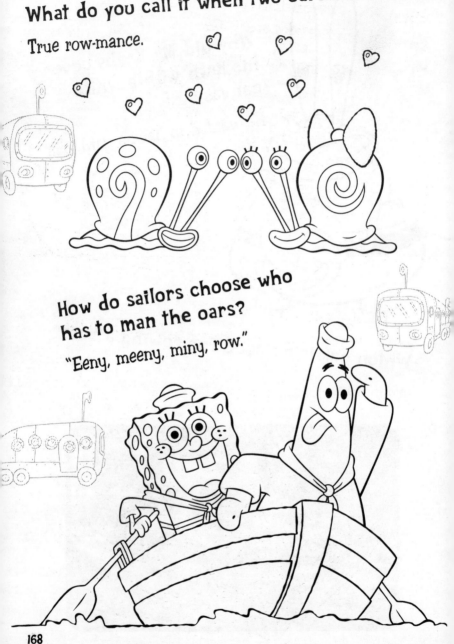

How do sailors choose who has to man the oars?

"Eeny, meeny, miny, row."

What happened to the spuds who went canoeing?

They became splashed potatoes.

Why do cars lie?

They can always get someone to back them up.

What does Mr. Krabs like to drive?

A hard bargain.

What kind of driving is SpongeBob best at?

Driving Squidward crazy.

What happened to the basketball player who took a vacation?

He was called for traveling.

Why do basketball players need cars?

So they can drive to the basket.

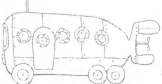

TEN
MINUTES
LATER

SpongeBob and Patrick were riding happily along when suddenly they heard a loud *klunk!* The bus rolled to a stop, and the driver got out to look under the hood. Smoke rose from the engine.

"Engine's busted," drawled the driver. "Looks like we're stuck."

"But the Jellyfishing Convention is about to start!" cried SpongeBob.

The driver pushed his hat back and scratched his forehead. "Well, it's not that much farther," he said. "You could walk."

Moments later SpongeBob and Patrick were trudging down the road with their backpacks. "I have an idea, Patrick. We could tell more jokes," SpongeBob suggested.

"Exactly what I was thinking," Patrick agreed, "except my idea had sandwiches in it."

Which part of a camera travels the fastest?

The zoom lens.

When is gasoline like the fish at Mussel Beach?

When it's pumped.

Which reptile is the best at reading maps?

The navigator.

What sign does Mr. Krabs always stop for?

The dollar sign.

When is a baseball team like a traveler looking for a bathroom?

When it needs a shortstop.

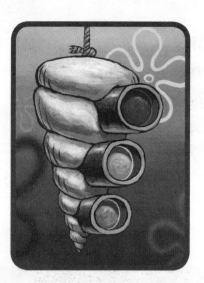

How is a cork like a traffic light?

They're both stoppers.

Why does SpongeBob refuse to turn left?

He always wants to do the right thing.

Why did the banana stick its hand out?

It was about to make a ripe turn.

Why does seawater always get to touch the shore First?

It has the right-of-wave.

Where do bees start their trips?

At the buzz station.

Which restaurant worker knows the most about transportation?

The busboy.

What do you call a tortoise with a camera?

A snapping turtle.

SNAP!

Why did the mummy pull off the road?

To go to the rest tomb.

TWO
DAYS
LATER

When SpongeBob and Patrick finally reached the Jellyfishing Convention, there was a long line to get in.

"Not another line!" Patrick wailed. "I'm tired of waiting!"

"Are you tired of jokes?" SpongeBob asked.

Patrick grinned. "Never! And I've got one for you. Knock, knock."

"Who's there?" answered SpongeBob.

"Turnip."

"Turnip who?"

"Turn up here, I need a rest stop," Patrick replied, as the two of them fell down laughing.

Why was Patrick chasing his clock?

It was running fast.

What kind of boat never sets sail?

A gravy boat.

S.S. CHEAPSKATE

Why was the sailor sad at the end of his voyage?

He missed the boat.

What do sailors eat for breakfast?

Boatmeal.

Why did the spud jump in the ocean?

He wanted to be a potato ship.

Why do old cars go on so many dates?

They're always getting fixed up.

What's a Krabby Patty's favorite way to travel?

Taking the fry way.

THE
NEXT
DAY

The next day SpongeBob and Patrick left the Jellyfishing Convention loaded down with souvenirs. "That was the greatest Annual Jellyfishing Convention ever!" SpongeBob exclaimed.

"Yeah!" Patrick agreed. "And the best part is now we don't have to take a long, boring bus ride back home!"

SpongeBob shook his head. "No, Patrick. We *do* have to take a long, boring bus ride back home! But it doesn't have to be boring!"

Patrick brightened up. "Jokes?" he asked hopefully.

"Of course!" SpongeBob answered, grinning.

Which part of the car is Patrick's Favorite?

The grub compartment.

Why did Plankton do a somersault on the windshield?

He wanted to roll down the window.

Why was Patrick afraid of taking the highway?

He heard you had to pay the troll.

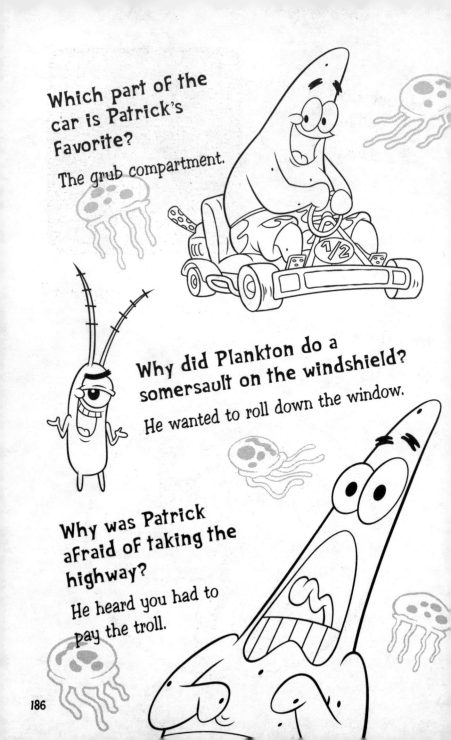

Where do chickens buy gas?

At a cluck stop.

Why did the mongoose pull off the highway?

He wanted to stop for a little snake.

What do you spread on a hot, toasty road?

Traffic jam.

Why did the top get in the car?

He wanted to go for a spin.

What has strings, a handle, and a powerful engine?

A tennis rocket.

What has four legs, white wool, and a powerful engine?

A rocket sheep.

What's the difference between Sandy in space and SpongeBob in water?

One goes into orbit and the other can absorb it.

What do teeth ride down the highway?

Molarcycles.

What do skunks ride down the highway?

Odorcycles.

At the end of the long bus ride SpongeBob and Patrick were finally back in Bikini Bottom. "Great trip, eh, buddy?" SpongeBob asked as they walked home.

"It sure was!" Patrick agreed.

"What was your favorite part?"

"The jokes!" Patrick shouted.

"You're right, Patrick," SpongeBob said. "And I've got one more for you: What did the pig say at the end of his trip?"

Patrick stared blankly. "There's no place like ham."

by David Lewman

What's big and lives in the water and works great on blackboards?

The Chalk Ness Monster.

Sandy: Why did Patrick punch the library?

SpongeBob: His teacher told him to hit the books.

SpongeBob: When is a postbox like the alphabet?

Squidward: When it's full of letters.

SpongeBob: What comes right after taking attendance?

Patrick: Taking an eleven dance.

Why did Mrs Puff become a teacher?

She's a classy lady.

Where did Sandy go before kindergarten?

Tree school.

Where did Squidward go before kindergarten?

Pre-scowl.

Mrs Puff: Why did the cow study all night?

Sandy: She wanted to go to the head of the grass.

Squidward: What did the drinking fountain say to the student?

SpongeBob: "Have a nice spray."

How does SpongeBob get to the second floor of the school?

He takes the square way.

You were right Spongebob! Those jokes are funny! Come on over to the Freedome tomorrow and celebrate. ♡ Sandy

Mr Krabs: What kind of ship must all students master?

Mrs Puff: Penmanship.

Patrick: What kind of pen is not good for writing?

Sandy: A pigpen.

SpongeBob: Why are skeletons so good at maths?

The Flying Dutchman: They really bone up on it.

Why did the student take lipstick and eye shadow to school?
He had to take a make-up test.

SpongeBob: What's the best kind of pen when you're lost in the desert?

Sandy: A fountain pen.

Why did Patrick hit the test with a tennis racket?

He wanted to ace the exam.

What did Mr Krabs say when he found an ancient bug in the dictionary?

"Why, that's the oldest tick in the book."

SpongeBob: Why wouldn't the teacher show his students how to connect two points?

Pearl: That's where he drew the line.

Did SpongeBob complete writing the letter *i* on time?
Yes, he finished right on the dot.

Patrick: Knock-knock.
Squidward: Who's there?
Patrick: Reese.
Squidward: Reese who?
Patrick: Recess is my favourite subject!

Patrick: Why was the soap always good in school?

SpongeBob: He never got in bubble.

Sandy: Where's the best place on a baseball field to take a test?

SpongeBob: Right field.

Mrs Puff: What comes just before detention?

Patrick: C-tention.

What kind of test does Bubble Buddy hate the most?

Pop quizzes.

SpongeBob: Which part of the beach is the smartest?

Pearl: The quicksand.

Sandy: Why did Patrick put his test in his piggy bank?

SpongeBob: He wanted to save it for a brainy day.

Patrick: Knock-knock.
SpongeBob: Who's there?
Patrick: Scram.
SpongeBob: Scram who?
Patrick: Let's cram for the big test tomorrow.

Why didn't Sponge-Bob study hard for his driver's license test?

He didn't want to start a traffic cram.

Patrick: Where do tests come from?

Mrs Puff: The Exami-Nation.

Squidward: What makes you think Mrs Puff finds you clever?

Patrick: She said I have a smart mouth.

Mrs Puff: Knock-knock.
SpongeBob: Who's there?
Mrs Puff: Ann, sir.
SpongeBob: Ann sir who?
Mrs Puff: Answer the question, SpongeBob!

What's the difference between someone who do-si-dos and an idea from SpongeBob's head?

One's a square dancer and the other's a squared answer!

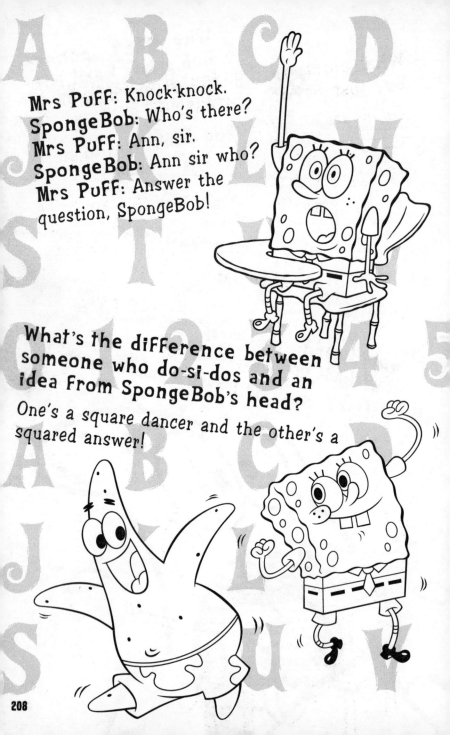

What electronic gadget did Patrick buy just before the big test?

An answering machine.

Sandy: What kind of answer doesn't belong in school?

Mrs Puff: A belly dancer!

SpongeBob: Why did the student write his maths homework on his toes?

Sandy: He was trying to think on his feet.

Why does Patrick think three, five, and seven are weird?

He heard they're odd numbers.

Why did Squidward sculpt a giant *A* out of clay?

He wanted to make the grade.

SpongeBob: What kind of test do they give in dancing school?

Squidward: True or waltz.

SpongeBob: What kind of test do they give in cooking school?

Mr Krabs: Multiple cheese.

Sandy: What's the difference between a trunk full of gold and a quiz on yellow cheese?

SpongeBob: One's a treasure chest and the other's a cheddar test.

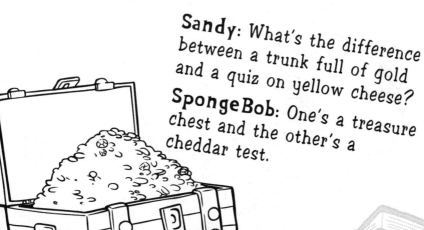

Why did SpongeBob bring a Fly to school?

For shoo-and-tell.

Patrick: If you fail an exam, is it a good idea to eat it?

SpongeBob: No, it would leave a bad test in your mouth.

SpongeBob: Why do phones always sit in the front of the class?

Squidward: They love to be called on.

Sandy: How did the chicken improve her grades?

SpongeBob: She joined a study coop.

Why did Patrick bring slime to school?

For a goop project.

Why did Plankton bring a ladder to school?

He wanted to get high grades.

SpongeBob: How do fish learn their grades?

Squidward: From a report carp.

What book does Mr Krabs hate to take out?

His cheque book.

215

What did Patrick learn at school?

His ABZzzzzzzzz's.

What does SpongeBob write his homework on when he's at the beach?

Sandpaper.

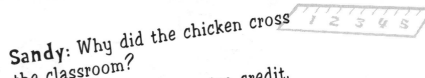

Sandy: Why did the chicken cross the classroom?

Mrs Puff: To get eggs-tra credit.

Why did Patrick bring lots of pencils to gym class?

He wanted to end up with the most points.

What book does Mr Krabs love to study?

His bankbook.

Why did one school bell always go off before the others?

It was the ringleader.

What did SpongeBob say when he realized he'd lost his oral report?

Nothing. He was speechless.

SpongeBob: Which fish is best in English class?

Mrs Puff: The grammarhead shark.

Why did SpongeBob's best friend take an apple to Mrs Puff?

He wanted to be teacher's Pat.

Why did Patrick build an extra room onto his rock?

His teacher told him to work on his addition.

Why did Patrick bring a seahorse to school?

He'd heard they were going to learn to read and ride.

What's the difference between a good student and Mr Krabs?

One knows how to read and the other's known for his greed.

Why did SpongeBob call his maths homework a "mystery"?

It just didn't add up.

Sandy: Did the flying fish study the lesson on waves?

Patrick: He skimmed it.

Mr Krabs: Why do swordfish get good grades?

SpongeBob: Because they're sharp

222

What did SpongeBob think of
Mr Krabs's lecture about pennies?

He couldn't make heads or tails
out of it.

When the teacher
asked him a question,
why did SpongeBob put
his hand in his mouth?

The answer was on the tip
of his tongue.

SpongeBob: How did the fish feel when school was cancelled?

Squidward: Like he was off the hook.

When does school turn Patrick's brain into a Fish?

When it makes his head swim.

Why did Patrick lie down on the classroom floor?

The teacher told him to lower his voice.

How did Mr Krabs get to know so much about the ocean?

He learned it from the Bikini Bottom up.

Why did SpongeBob climb up to the classroom ceiling?

The teacher told him to speak up.

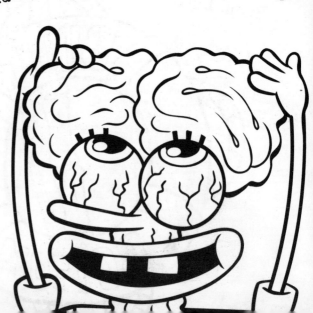

Why did SpongeBob wrap sheets and blankets around his brain?

The teacher told him to make up his mind.

Squidward: Why don't cows get exact answers in maths?

Sandy: They're always rounding up.

Why did Squidward spend hours talking about just one painting?

He wanted his students to get the picture.

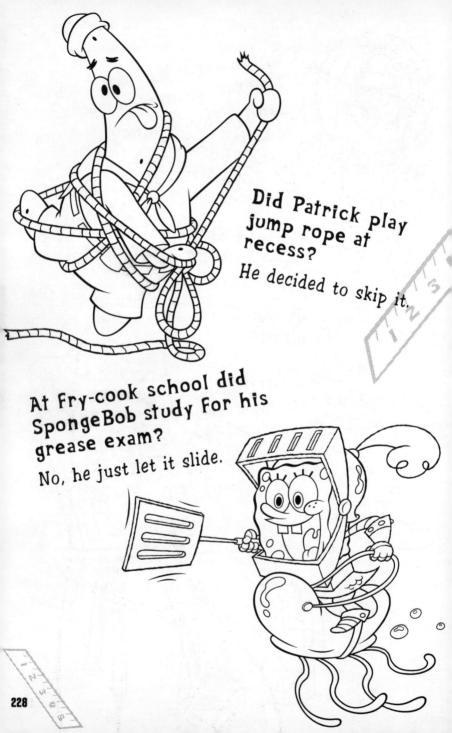

Did Patrick play jump rope at recess?

He decided to skip it.

At Fry-cook school did SpongeBob study for his grease exam?

No, he just let it slide.

SpongeBob: Why don't astronauts make good students?

Sandy: They keep spacing out.

Why did Patrick bring frozen orange juice to class?

The teacher told him he needed to concentrate.

Why did Plankton steal his chair from school?

The teacher told him to take his seat.

SpongeBob: What did the ghost get on his exam?

The Flying Dutchman: A Boo minus.

Squidward: What's the worst kind of B to get on your homework?

Patrick: A bumblebee.

What's the difference between Patrick on a seesaw and Patrick looking at his report card?

The first seesaws and the second saw C's.

What did Patrick say when he saw the teacher marking his test?

"Go ahead, make my D!"

SpongeBob: When is a D not a bad grade?
Sandy: When it's a chickadee.

Sandy: What did the dog get on his test?

Mr Krabs: An arf.

if Plankton were a grade, what grade would he be?

A-menace.

233

Patrick: Where do polar bears go after kindergarten?

SpongeBob: Frost grade.

Why did Patrick let his maths book Fall on the Floor?

He wanted to drop the subject.

Sandy: Which grade is over the quickest?

Mrs PuFF: Second grade.

Where did Sandy go after second grade?

Furred grade.

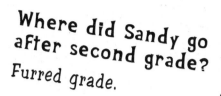

Where do bacteria have P. E. class?

In the germnasium.

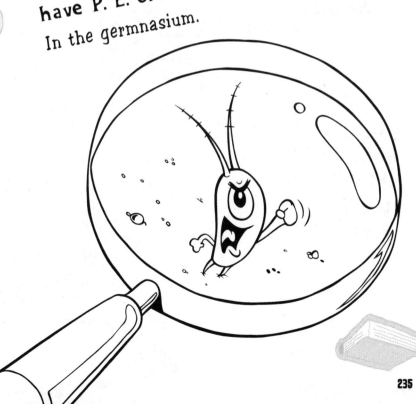

Which kind of musical note is Mr Krabs's favourite?

The quarter note.

Why did Patrick do his maths homework on SpongeBob's back?

SpongeBob said Patrick could always count on him.

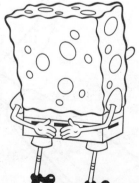

Why did Patrick hand in his test before he'd finished?

He ran out of guess.

Squidward: Was the school nurse willing to treat the sick sea monster?

Patrick: She said she'd give it a shot.

Why did SpongeBob do his school exercises over and over and over?

He wanted to be king of the drill.

What's Mr Krabs's favourite kind of test?

Fill-in-the-bank.

SpongeBob: Why do pirates make bad students?

Mr Krabs: Everything goes in one ahrrrr and out the other.

Patrick: Knock-knock.
SpongeBob: Who's there?
Patrick: Miss.
SpongeBob: Miss who?
Patrick: Mistakes are really easy to make.

Why can't Patrick divide by two?

He doesn't know the half of it.

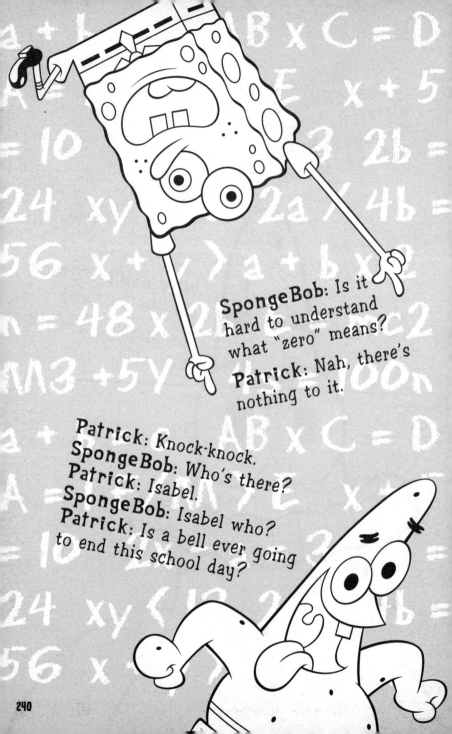

SpongeBob: Is it hard to understand what "zero" means?

Patrick: Nah, there's nothing to it.

Patrick: Knock-knock.
SpongeBob: Who's there?
Patrick: Isabel.
SpongeBob: Isabel who?
Patrick: Is a bell ever going to end this school day?

A Pirate Joke Book

by David Lewman

What did the pirates do when SpongeBob asked to join them?

They welcomed him with open ahrrs.

Pearl: Who steers the ship while the captain naps?

Sandy: His co-pirate.

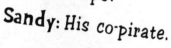

Who helped SpongeBob find his missing treasure?

A pirate detective.

Ahrr!

Patrick: What's a pirate's favorite holiday?

SpongeBob: Ahrrbor Day.

Ahrr!

Ahrr!

Mrs. Puff: Which pirate is the most musical?

Mr. Krabs: Sing-along John Silver.

Squidward: Which pirate is the sleepiest?

Patrick: Long Yawn Silver.

Patrick: Why did the pirate go up in a hot-air balloon?

Squidward: He heard every cloud has a silver lining.

Pearl: Which pirate is the messiest?

SpongeBob: Long John Spiller.

247

Squidward: Which pirate loves to eat?

SpongeBob: Snackbeard.

Squidward: Why did the pirate send her sword to school?

Sandy: She wanted it to be sharp.

Sandy: What's the difference between a pirate present and a runaway pumpkin?

Squidward: One's a gift sword, and the other's a swift gourd.

Pearl: Why did the pirate cut off his beard when the clouds rolled in?

SpongeBob: He was shaving it for a rainy day.

Why was the Flying Dutchman looking for clues?

He was on a treasure haunt.

Mr. Krabs: What's a pirate's favorite state?

Sandy: Ahrrkansas.

SpongeBob: What's a pirate's favorite sport?

Patrick: Ahrrchery.

Mr. Krabs: Why did the bug crawl up the pirate's sword?

Plankton: It wanted to get to the point.

Squidward: What is a pirate's favorite nut?

Sandy: The chestnut.

Patrick: How do pirates find buried chests without a map?

SpongeBob: They go on a treasure hunch.

Mr. Krabs: Knock-knock.

SpongeBob: Who's there?

Mr. Krabs: Sherlock.

SpongeBob: Sherlock who?

Mr. Krabs: Sure, lock the chest — it's full of treasure!

Sandy: Did the pirate really open the locked chest just by singing a song?

Patrick: Yes, she sang in the right key.

Squidward: What did the pirates do to the electric eel?

Plankton: They made him shock the plank.

Mr. Krabs: How did the pirate clean the golden floor?

SpongeBob: With a treasure mop.

Patrick: Why do pirate flags wave?

SpongeBob: To say hello!

SpongeBob: Why are pirate flags always grouchy?

Sandy: Because they have crossbones.

255

Mrs. Puff: Who wears an eye patch, a wooden leg, and a chest protector?

SpongeBob: An umpirate.

Ahrr!

Ahrr!

Patrick: What do you get when you cross a parrot and an elephant?

Painty the Pirate: I don't know, but I wouldn't want it sitting on my shoulder!

Ahrr!

SpongeBob: What kind of jokes do parrots tell?

Mr. Krabs: Squawk-squawk jokes.

Ahrr!

Ahrr!

Ahrr!

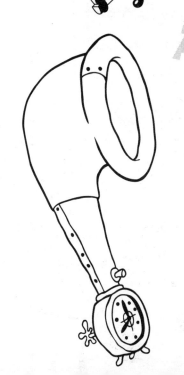

SpongeBob: What do parrots use to wake up in the morning?

Squidward: An alarm squawk.

Ahrr!

Patchy the Pirate: What did the pirate name his wooden-legged horse?

Painty the Pirate: Peg-asus!

Sandy: Why was the parrot mad at the pirate?

Pearl: Because he gave her the cold shoulder.

SpongeBob: Did the parrot study for his flying exam?

Mrs. Puff: No, he just winged it.

Patrick: Did the old parrot help the young parrot?

SpongeBob: Yes, he took him under his wing.

SpongeBob: Who wears an eye patch, says "ahrrr," and hunts for fossils?

Squidward: An ahrrchaeologist!

Squidward: What's a parrot's favorite holiday?

Plankton: Feather's Day.

Why is Painty the Pirate stuck in a Frame?

He's a work of ahrrt.

SpongeBob: Why did the pirate tie a piece of fruit to his face?

Mr. Krabs: He wanted to wear an eye peach.

SpongeBob: Where do pirates play pinball?

Patrick: The ahrrcade!

SpongeBob: What's a pirate's best basketball move?

Patrick: His hook shot.

Squidward: Who designs pirates' houses?

Mr. Krabs: Ahrrchitects!

Patrick: What kind of bees do pirates like?

Mr. Krabs: Rubies!

Sandy: What is a pirate's favorite fish?

SpongeBob: The goldfish.

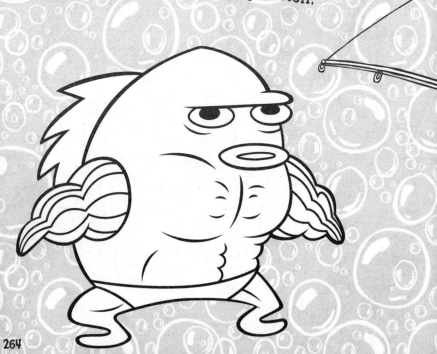

SpongeBob: Why does the pirate go to the jeweler every year?

Squidward: To have his earring tested.

Why did Painty the Pirate stop talking to Patchy the Pirate?

They had a big ahrrgument.

Ahrr!

Ahrr!

Ahrr!

Plankton: Which ocean is the pirate's favorite?

SpongeBob: The Ahrrctic Ocean.

Squidward: What's a pirate's best boxing punch?

Plankton: A right hook.

Ahrr!

Is Painty the Pirate guilty of bad singing?

No, he was framed.

Ahrr!

Patrick: Why do monkeys climb on pirates?

SpongeBob: To steal their bandanas.

When Patchy the Pirate's parrot got grouchy, why did Patrick try to eat him?

He'd heard he was a crabby Potty.

SpongeBob: What do pirate ships wear to look scary?

Squidward: Halloween masts.

SpongeBob: What bird is the pirate's favorite?

Sandy: The goldfinch.

Patrick: Where do pirates keep their eggs?

Mr. Krabs: In the crow's nest.

SpongeBob: Which part of a pirate ship is the smelliest?

Patrick: The poop deck.

Which part of a pirate ship is Mr. Krabs's favorite?

The quarterdeck.

Squidward: What dive do pirates like to do?

Patrick: The cannonball!

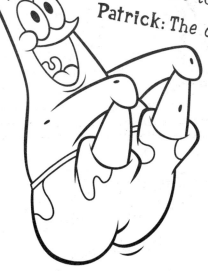

Was SpongeBob ready to be shot out of the pirates' cannon?

Yes, he was really on the ball.

Plankton: What did the big cannon say at the celebration?

Mr. Krabs: "Business is booming!"

Patchy the Pirate: What's the difference between a ghost and a cannon?

Painty the Pirate: One likes to *boo* and the other likes to *boom*.

Did Patrick do a good job of loading the cannon?

No, he dropped the ball.

Why did Patrick try to play music on the crate the cannon came in?

He'd heard it was a boom box.

Squidward: What happened when the cannon asked the pirates to stop using him?

Mr. Krabs: He was fired.

Patrick: What game do cannons like to play?

Plankton: Fuseball.

Sandy: Did the cannon have fun on his birthday?

SpongeBob: Yes, he had a blast!

What did the angry pirate do when Patrick accidentally lit the cannon?

He blew a fuse.

Patrick: What do pirates use to keep their boots on?

Sandy: Swashbuckles.

SpongeBob: How did the pirate do on his boating test?

Mrs. Puff: He sailed through it.

Mrs. Puff: Why did the pirates spread their wares out on the deck?

Mr. Krabs: They were holding a garage sail.

SpongeBob: Which pirate has a big beard, a gold earring, and six legs?

Patrick: Captain Squidward.

Why did Patrick kneel down and put his palms on the pirate boat?

Someone yelled, "All hands on deck!"

Why did SpongeBob dig for treasure under the chicken coop?

He heard that *eggs* mark the spot.

Painty the Pirate: Why did the anchor stop trying to reach the sea floor?

Patchy the Pirate: He was at the end of his rope.

SpongeBob: Was the pirate wrong to forget to pack any rope?

Mr. Krabs: Yes, he was way out of line.

Ahrr!

Ahrr!

Ahrr!

Ahrr!

Sandy: Why did the pirate climb into the ship's rigging with a book?

Squidward: He wanted to read between the lines.

Ahrr!

SpongeBob: What do pirates wear under their pants?

Patrick: Their plunderwear.

Ahrr!
Ahrr!

Patrick: What did the angry pirate do when he found out his ship was overloaded?

Squidward: He went through the reef.

Squidward: What do you call four pirate ships that sink in the same spot?

Mrs. Puff: A wreck-tangle.

Mrs. Puff: Why did the pirate make his crew study?

SpongeBob: He was hoping for a scholarship.

Why did SpongeBob smack his ship's floor?

He thought the pirate told him to swat the deck.

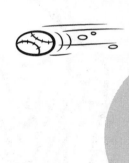

Sandy: Why do pirates like to play baseball?

Plankton: They love to steal bases.

Patrick: What would Santa Claus say if he was a pirate?

Squidward: "Yo-ho-ho-ho!"

SpongeBob: What do pirates do when they can't sleep?

Mr. Krabs: Count ships.

Sandy: When is a pirate like a bird?
Plankton: When he's a-robbin'.

SpongeBob: What is the pirate's favorite bedtime story?

Patrick: "Sleeping Booty."

Shiver me timbers!

We're at the end of the book!